Galliards, Pavans and Other Keyboard Works

Selections from the Fitzwilliam Virginal Book

by William Byrd, John Bull, and Others

Edited by J.A. Fuller Maitland and W. Barclay Squire
and revised by Blanche Winogron

DOVER PUBLICATIONS, INC.
Mineola, New York

Bibliographical Note

This Dover edition, first published in 2004, is a new selection of works from
*The Fitzwilliam Virginal Book / Edited from the Original Manuscript with an
Introduction and Notes by J.A. Fuller Maitland and W. Barclay Squire / Revised
Dover Edition / Corrected, Edited and with a Preface by Blanche Winogron,*
Dover Publications, New York, 1980. The present introductory note has been
adapted from that edition and from Thomas Morley's *A Plaine and Easie
Introduction to Practicall Musicke*, London, 1597.

International Standard Book Number: 0-486-43120-7

Manufactured in the United States of America
Dover Publications, Inc., 31 East 2nd Street, Mineola, N.Y. 11501

CONTENTS BY COMPOSER

The works are presented in the order in which they appeared in the original Fitzwilliam Virginal Book.

CONTENTS BY TITLE

For ease of reference, titles above have been standardized in accordance with The New Grove Dictionary of Music and Musicians, 1980.

The roman numerals give each piece's index number in the complete Fitzwilliam Virginal Book.

In the history of musical notation, there is no more important document than the Fitzwilliam Virginal Book. Transcribed from MSS. of widely different dates and degrees of correctness, by one writer, the pieces, which range from about 1550 to 1620, are so varied in style that almost all the resources of the time, as regards the writing down of music, must have been exhausted. The period is a peculiarly interesting one, since it marks the point when the old systems of musical theory, as well as of musical notation, were beginning to give place to those which are now observed, and when the modern laws were only in a very incomplete stage of their development. Many of the difficulties encountered by the writer of the MS. were evidently not reduced to rules, and fairly often we find him trying new experiments in the indication of accidentals, and in other similar points. The regular system of bars with which music has been familiar since the middle of the 17th century, was only in its infancy; still, in general terms it may be said that the use of bars was so clearly a foreshadowing of the present system, that it has not been found necessary to alter the original barring, although in certain cases, dotted bars have been employed to make the difficult passages clearer for the modern musician. The time-signatures present an arrangement that can hardly be made clear without supplementary signs, and accordingly these are among the very few additions made by the editors. Various points connected with the use of accidentals, ornaments, etc. are more fully dealt with below.

THE MODES. The essential difference between the music of the period at which the Virginal Book was written and all that we are accustomed to hear in the present day, lies in the influence which was still exercised by the ecclesiastical modes. The composers of the beginning of the XVIIth century were undoubtedly freeing themselves gradually from the strict modal limitations observed by their predecessors, but they still recognized fully the different characteristics of the ancient scales, and were only dimly conscious of the possibilities opened out by the fusion of the Ionian, Lydian, and Mixolydian modes into our present major scale, and that of the Æolian, Dorian, Phrygian into our present minor. A very large majority of the compositions in the collection are easily referable to one or other of the modes, and it would be in almost all instances incorrect to speak of them as in such and such a key. Specimens of nearly all the ecclesiastical modes are to be found in the collection, but those most usual are the Dorian, Mixolydian, Æolian, and Ionian, with their plagal counterparts. The Phrygian and Lydian occur most rarely. The presence of a flat in the signature does not mean, as it would in the present day, that the key of F major or D minor is

intended; but that the mode, whatever it may be, is transposed a fourth above its normal place. The process known as "double transposition" yields two flats in the signature. It is most necessary to bear in mind the modal character of the music in playing compositions in the Mixolydian mode, which seem to be in the key of G, but without a sharp in the signature: in these F natural is only too easily mistaken for F sharp.

ACCIDENTALS. Closely allied to the modal influence, and indeed due to it in a large degree, is the use of accidentals. In modes which had no "leading tone" a semitone below the tonic or final of the mode, such as the Dorian, Phrygian, Mixolydian, and Æolian, the singers in earlier days were required to introduce accidental notes to supply the want, and without the employment of the written signs which are now in use. The unwritten laws of "musica ficta" must have led to a great amount of confusion when the performers were not fully experienced, and as music became more elaborate, and the instinctive desire for modulation became stronger, written accidentals had to be inserted. But it was long before the rule now in force was established. It seems not to have been absolutely binding that the first flat or sharp in the bar should be so marked, nor was it understood that this first accidental ruled all the notes of the same pitch until the end of the bar, when a new accidental must be introduced. On the one hand, we find many instances of a sharp omitted before the first note to which it obviously refers, and on the other, it is placed before every repetition of the note, even in the same bar. This carelessness, or rather want of system in regard to accidentals, makes many passages ambiguous which would otherwise be perfectly clear; and the editors have been compelled, in many pieces, to supply accidentals which can be only matters of conjecture, and upon which each reader must form his own conclusions. Interpolated accidentals are indicated in all cases by being placed above or below the notes to which they refer, and by being enclosed in brackets.

Sometimes a flat or, more rarely, a sharp, is placed at the beginning of a bar, although the note to which it applies may not be the first of the bar; here it is clear that the accidental governs all the notes of the same pitch in the bar, just as in more modern music.

The restoration of a note previously altered by an accidental, by means of a flat or sharp, contradicting a sharp or flat (of course the sign now in use for a natural is of far later origin), is of very rare occurrence; and in the great majority of cases this restoration has been made conjecturally. In dealing with such passages, the character of the mode employed must be borne in mind, and help may often be got by comparing the reading of similar sections, repeated with or without ornamentation.

ORNAMENTS. The two ornaments in most common use are 𝄋 and 𝄌. The first apparently indicates a slide of a third upwards, or a double appoggiatura, and possible occasionally a mordent; the second seems to be used for a long or short shake, or for either a "Pralltriller" or "Mordent." A third sign seems to be employed in very rare instances, figured thus: 𝄋 but it seems probable that the sign is simply a canceling or correction of the sign 𝄋 wrongly put in.

BARRING. It is necessary, in order to understand the system on which the bars are used in the MS., to remember that the bars are entirely independent of the time-signature. This latter has only to do with the proportional values of the notes to each other; the bars are merely, at this period, a convenient help to the player's eye, and although they usually follow the rhythmic outline of the composition pretty closely, yet they are often very irregular. When a piece begins with long-held notes each bar contains three or four times as much as the bars in the later part of the piece do, when the ornaments are more rapid. As a general rule it seems that the pieces have the longer bars at the beginning rather than at the end.

The writer's use of double bars, or rather of the repeat marks which usually accompany the double bars, is not quite clear. In the first part of the MS. almost every section seems to be marked for repetition, but as the dots are generally omitted in the later pieces, it may be that they are only ornamental. They have been retained exactly as they stand in the MS. and the reader must use his discretion as to their interpretation.

DIVISION OF SECTIONS. Closely allied to the double bars is the system of marking off the various sections of the pieces. The simplest arrangement is that employed in sets of variations where the method of numbering is identical with the modern practice. In some of the more elaborate dance-measures and elsewhere the tune itself is in two sections; in this case the latter half, both of the tune and of the variations, is marked with a small figure 2, the larger figures appearing over the first section of each variation. In the case of a piece where each separate section is at once presented in an ornamental shape, the abbreviation "Rep." is used; this seems always to indicate the ornamented version of a simple strain just preceding it. The numeration of many of the fantasias in which a rudimentary fugal structure is apparent, follows the successive entries of the theme or answer.

J.A. FULLER MAITLAND AND W. BARCLAY SQUIRE

TAKEN FROM
A Plaine and Easie Introduction to Practicall Musicke, 1597

The most principal and chiefest kind of music which is made without a ditty is the FANTASY, that is when a musician taketh a point at his pleasure and wresteth and turneth it as he list, making either much or little of it according as shall seem best in his own conceit. In this may more art be shown than in any other music because the composer is tied to nothing, but that he may add, diminish, and alter at his pleasure. And this kind will bear any allowances whatsoever tolerable in other music except changing the air and leaving the key, which in Fantasie may never be suffered. Other things you may use at your pleasure, bindings with discords, quick motions, slow motions, Proportions, and what you list.

The next in gravity and goodness unto this is called a PAVAN, a kind of staid music ordained for grave dancing and most commonly made of three strains, whereof every strain is played or sung twice; a strain they make to contain eight, twelve, or sixteen semibreves as they list, yet fewer than eight I have not seen in any Pavan. In this you may not so much insist in following the point as in a Fantasy, but it shall be enough to touch it once and so away to some close. Also in this you must cast your music by four, so that if you keep that rule it is no matter how many fours you put in your strain for it will fall out well enough in the end, the art of dancing being come to that perfection that every reasonable dancer will make measure of no measure, so that it is no great matter of what number you make your strain.

After every Pavan we usually set a GALLIARD (that is a kind of music made out of the other), causing it go by a measure which the learned call *trochaicam rationem,* consisting of a long and short stroke successively, for as the foot *trochaeus* consisteth of one syllable of two times and another of one time, so is the first of these two strokes double to the latter, the first being in time of a semibreve and the latter of a minim. This is a brighter and more stirring kind of dancing than the Pavan, consisting of the same number of strains; and look how many fours of semibreves you put in the strain of your Pavan, so many times six minims must you put in the strain of your Galliard.

The ALMAN is a more heavy dance than this (fitly representing the nature of the people whose name it carrieth) so that no extraordinary motions are used in dancing of it. It is made of strains, sometimes two, sometimes three, and every strain is made by four; but you must mark that the four of the Pavan measure is in Dupla Proportion to the four of the Alman measure, so that as the usual Pavan containeth in a strain the time of sixteen semibreves, so the usual Alman containeth the time of eight, and most commonly in short notes.

Like unto this (but more light) be the VOLTES and COURANTES which being both of a measure are, notwithstanding, danced after sundry fashions, the Volte rising and leaping, the Courante travising and running, in which measure also our Country Dance is made, though it be danced after another form than any of the former. All these be made in strains, either two or three as shall seem best to the maker, but the Courante hath twice so much in a strain as the English Country Dance.

There be also many other kinds of dances, as Hornpipes, jigs, and infinite more which I cannot nominate unto you, but knowing these the rest cannot but be understood as being one with some of these which I have already told you. And as there are divers kinds of music so will some men's humours be more inclined to one kind than to another; as some will be good descanters and excel in descant and yet will be but bad composers, others will be good composers and but bad descanters extempore upon a plainsong; some will excel in composition of Motets and being set or enjoined to make a Madrigal will be very far from the nature of it; likewise some will be so possessed with the Madrigal humour as no man may be compared with them in that kind and yet being enjoined to compose a Motet or some sad and heavy music will be far from the excellency which they had in their own vein. Lastly some will be so excellent in points of voluntary upon an instrument as one would think it impossible for him not to be a good composer and yet being enjoined to make a song will do it so simply as one would think a scholar of one year's practice might easily compose a better. And I dare boldly affirm that look which is he who thinketh himself the best descanter of all his neighbours, enjoin him to make but a Scottish jig, he will grossly err in the true nature and quality of it.

THOMAS MORLEY

Galliards, Pavans and Other Keyboard Works

Selections from the Fitzwilliam Virginal Book

Jhon come kisse me now.

WILLIAM BYRD.

4

6

15.

16.

WILLIAM BYRD.

Robin.

JOHN MUNDAY.

10

JHON MUNDAY.

* The sign :S: occurs here in the same position in the MS.

The Irishe Ho-Hoane.

ANON.

Pavane.

F. RICHARDSON.

* Semiquavers in M.S.

11

12

FERDINANDO RICHARDSON.

The Quadran Pavan.

JOHN BULL.

* A third higher in the M.S.   ** D in M.S.   *** A in M.S.   **** C in M.S.   ***** Semiquavers in the M.S.

20

8.

DOCTOR BULL.

$\begin{smallmatrix}B\\G\\E\end{smallmatrix}$ in M.S.   ** C B in M.S.   *** D in M.S.

Galiard to the Quadran Pavan.

JOHN BULL.

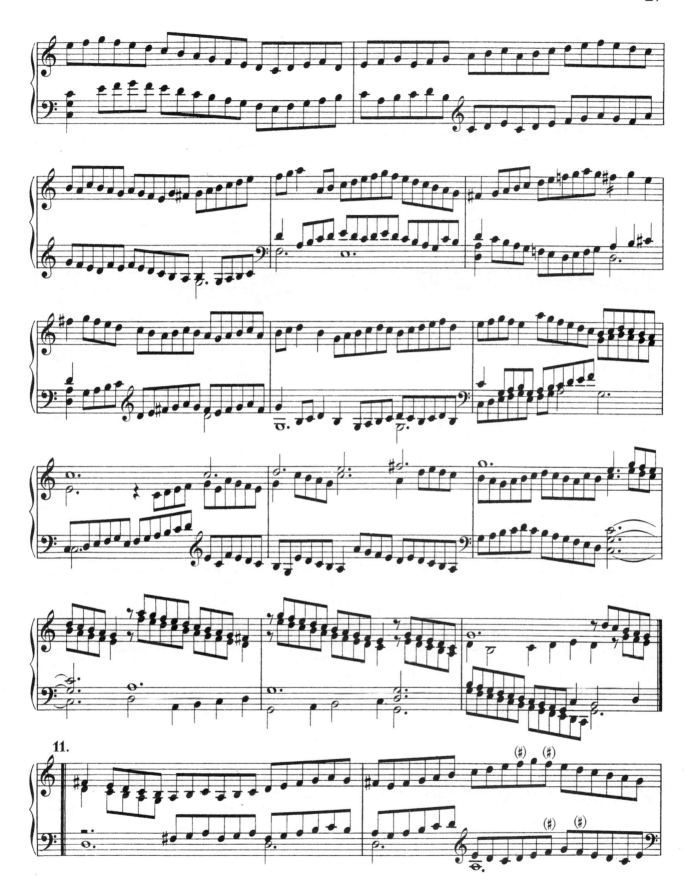

11.

28

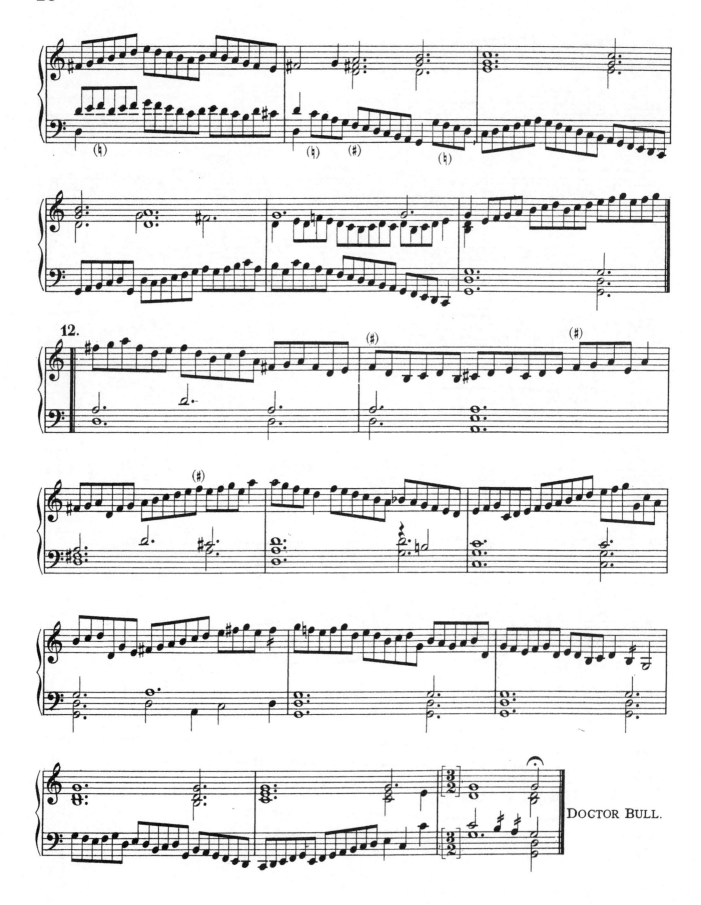

DOCTOR BULL.

The woods so wilde.*

ORLANDO GIBBONS.

* The piece breaks off, after the first two bars of section 5, a the rest of the page being left blank; the latter part of the composition is here supplied, from a copy in the British Museum, (Add. MSS. 31,403, fol. 21–23.) It is there ascribed to Orlando Gibbons, and in the early sections several very slight differences exist between the two MSS. mostly in the matter of ornaments.

** Quavers in M.S.

30

Add. MS. 31, 403 fol. 21-23.

* The MS has a natural to the B.

33

Mr ORLANDO GIBBONS.

Goe from my window.*

JOHN MUNDAY.

---

* A virtually identical composition appears elsewhere in the Fitzwilliam Virginal Book, where it is attributed to Thomas Morley; variation 8 is unique to the present version.

36

38

JHON MUNDAY.

* C in M S.

Ut, re, mi, fa, sol, la.

JOHN BULL.

* This interesting experiment in enharmonic modulation is thus tentatively expressed in the M.S.; the passage proves that some kind of "equal temperament" must have been employed at this date.

* In the manuscript written a third too low.

42

* Minim in M.S.

DOCTOR BULL.

* Minim in M. S.

The Carmans Whistle.

WILLIAM BYRD.

*D in M.S.

46

WILLIAM BYRD.

* The notes from * to * are a third higher in the M.S.

The Hunt's up.

WILLIAM BYRD.

* Crotchet rest in M.S.

50

* C in the MS.

7.

52

12.

WILLIAM BYRD.

*G in M.S.

O Mistris Myne.

WILLIAM BYRD.

* C sharp in M.S.

58

* Semiquavers in M. S.   *—* A crotchet and quaver in M. S.

* Crotchet in M. S.

60

WILLIAM BYRD.

* Quavers in M. S.

Pavana Pagget.

PETER PHILIPS.

63

* D in M.S.　　　** A F in M.S.

64

Rep.

PEETER PHILIPS.

Galiarda.

PETER PHILIPS.

66

Rep.

PEETER PHILIPS.

Pauana Doloroso.

SET BY PETER PHILIPS.

70

72

74

PETER PHILIPS 1593.

Galiarda Dolorosa.

PETER PHILIPS.

76

* Quaver in M. S.   ** C in M. S.

PETER PHILIPS.

Amarilli di Julio Romano.

PETER PHILIPS.

* B in M. S.

(b)

(b)

(b)

* In the original madrigal this F is sharp.

** F in the M.S.

Rep.

PETER PHILIPS 1603.

Fantasia.

JOHN BULL.

*A in M. S.

DOCTOR BULL.

Felix namque.

Thomas Tallis.

90

92

* A in the M.S.

THOMAS TALLIS. 1562.

Pavana Lachrymæ.

John Dowland, set by Byrd.

96

* The middle note of this chord is F in the M S.

JHON DOWLAND, sett
foorth by WILLIAM BYRD.

Galiarda.

JAMES HARDING, set by BYRD.

102

Rep.

JAMES HARDING, sett
foorth by WILLIAM BYRD.

Fantasia.

T. MORLEY.

103

104

* A change of clef is omitted here.

THOMAS MORLEY.

* The middle note of this chord is G in the M.S.

The Quadran Paven.

WILLIAM BYRD.

* These two bars, the text of which is evidently corrupt, have been corrected from the version given in Will. Forster's Virginal Book in the Buckingham-Palace library.

* See note p. III.

* Semiquavers in the M.S.

** The notes in brackets are indicated by "directs" in the previous line; they are not in the M.S.

116

* C sharp in the M. S.

117

WILLIAM
BYRD.

* G in the M. S.   ** This bar is left blank in the M. S; it is supplied from Will. Forster's M. S.

Galiard to the Quadran Paven.

WILLIAM BYRD.

Rep.

* Demisemiquavers in the M. S.

* Demisemiquavers in the M.S.

* C sharp in the M.S.

122

WILLIAM
BYRD.

Dr. Bull's Juell.

124

Rosasolis.

GILES FARNABY.

GILES
FARNABY.

The New Sa-Hoo.

GILES FARNABY.

GILES FARNABY.

*- - * Demisemiquavers in the MS.   * A in the M.S.

Alman.

Thomas Morley.

THOMAS MORLEY.

Wolseys Wilde.

WILLIAM BYRD.

WILLIAM BYRD.

Callino Casturame.

WILLIAM BYRD.

La Volta.

T. MORLEY [set by] WILLIAM BYRD.

WILLIAM BYRD.

The Irishe Dumpe.

ANON.

Watkins Ale.

ANON.

138

A Gigg.

WILLIAM BYRD.

WILLIAM BYRD.

* B in MS.

Can shee.

ANON.

A Gigge.

Doctor Bull's my selfe.

DOCTOR BULL.

A Gigge.

JOHN BULL.

DOCTOR BULL.

Sr. Jhon Grayes Galiard.

W. B.*

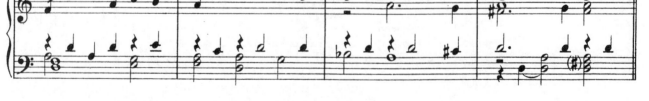

* W. B. indicates William Byrd, but this is now known to be a wrongful attribution.

Preludium.

JOHN BULL.

W. B.

DOCTOR BULL.

A Toy.

ANON.

Rep.

Rep.

Giles Farnaby's Dreame.

* Semiquaver in the M.S.

GILES FARNABY.

His Rest.
Galiard.

GILES FARNABY.

GILES FARNABIE.

His Humour.

GILES FARNABY.

GILES FARNABY.

*A in the M.S.

An Almain.

ANON.

Corranto.

ANON.

Alman.

ANON.

Corranto.

ANON.

Corranto.

ANON.

Corranto.

ANON.

Daunce.

ANON.

* F sharp in the M.S.

Worster Braules.

THOMAS TOMKINS.

THOMAS TOMKINS.

Fantasia.

GILES FARNABY.

* B flat in the M.S.

152

GILES FARNABYE.

* A in the M.S.

Loth to Depart.

GILES FARNABY.

* G in the M.S.

156

GILES FARNABY.

* Demisemiquavers in the M.S.

The Primerose.

MARTIN PEERSON.

Rep.

* Quavers in the M.S.

MARTIN PEERSON.

157

The Fall of the Leafe.

MARTIN PEERSON.

MARTIN PEERSON.

158

Farnabye's Conceit.

GILES FARNABYE.

Allemanda.

ANON.

Rep.

* D sharp in the M.S.

160

Why aske you.

GILES FARNABY.

* Crotchet in the M. S.

164

Rep.

(#) (#)

2

Rep.

(#)

GILES FARNABY.

*E in the M S.

Pavana.

Orlando Gibbons.

166

ORLANDO GIBBONS.